G000160405

The Crow Family Book

by Jane Russ

GRAFFEG

Contents

Introduction

Above: Author and crow.

When this project was first on the schedule in approximately 2018, we were going to call it *The Corvid Book*. Subsequently, after the pandemic hit, we thought this might be open to misreading and so we reverted to *The Crow Family Book*.

I shall only be looking in detail at the crow family found on these islands but there are in fact 45 members worldwide.

The ultimate 'Marmite' bird, you either love them or hate them but either way, nobody ever disputes that the one thread running through all descriptions of them all is their intelligence. I will be discussing and explaining this in the first chapter and I hope that these amazing creatures will capture your imagination the way that they have captured mine.

My first interaction with these awe-inspiring birds is documented in this photograph taken in 1957 and I have been enthralled by them ever since.

UK Corvids

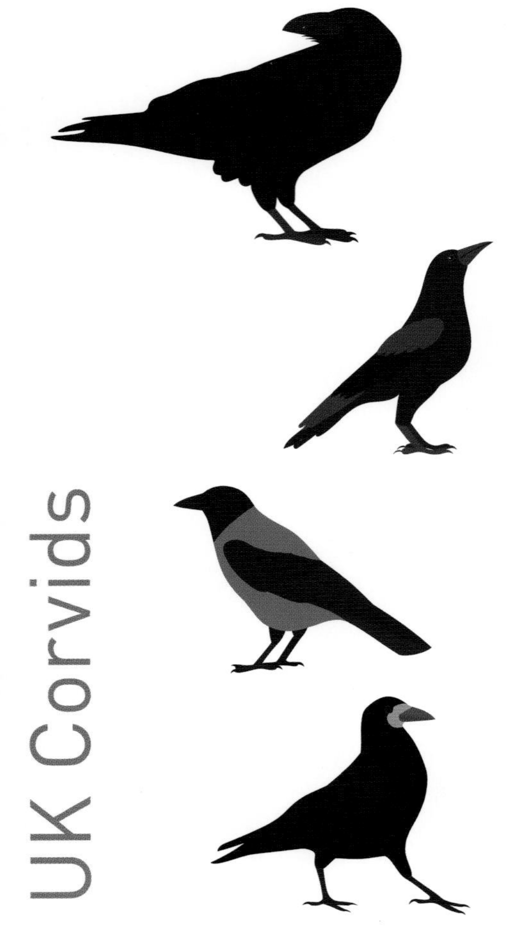

Raven

Scientific name: *Corvus corax*
Length: 60-68cm
Wingspan: 120-150cm
Weight: 800-1,500g

Carrion crow

Scientific name: *Corvus corone*
Length: 45-47cm
Wingspan: 93-104cm
Weight: 370-650g

Hooded crow

Scientific name: *Corvus cornix*
Length: 45-47cm
Wingspan: 93-104cm
Weight: 370-650g

Rook

Scientific name: *Corvus frugilegus*
Length: 44-46cm
Wingspan: 81-99cm
Weight: 280-340g

Magpie

Scientific name: *Pica pica*
Length: 44-46cm
Wingspan: 52-60cm
Weight: 200-250g

Chough

Scientific name: *Pyrrhocorax pyrrhocorax*
Length: 39-40cm
Wingspan: 73-90cm
Weight: 260-350g

Jackdaw

Scientific name: *Corvus monedula*
Length: 34cm
Wingspan: 70cm
Weight: 220g

Jay

Scientific name: *Garrulus glandarius*
Length: 34-35cm
Wingspan: 52-58cm
Weight: 140-190g

Jackdaw

Not Such a Bird Brain

Not Such a Bird Brain

There seems only one place to start when discussing corvids: how clever they are and why the term 'bird brain' in this instance is a complete misnomer.

The subject is massive and this book is not meant to be a definitive exploration of the brainpower of corvids: that is a book in itself. Here I hope you will find a taster into that world to hook you into your own research and inspire you to broaden your knowledge of the subject.

Let us start with the fact that the brain to bodyweight ratio in crows and ravens is close to that of mammals and primates and far above that of other birds except large parrots and macaws. In his book *In the Company of Crows and Ravens*, illustrated by Tony Angell, Professor John Marzluff, an eminent wildlife scientist from the University of Washington, states: 'Mentally, crows and ravens are more like flying monkeys than they are like other birds.'

The graph on the right (with permission from Tony Angell) illustrates the brain to body ratio. The solid line represents the fixed weight of primates, mammals and birds and the dots show where each of the birds comes in relation to their brain size. It is easy to see that ravens and crows are closer to primates and that the other corvids are mainly closer to mammals. Both are way above other birds, apart from the blue and gold and the green-winged macaws, who are the avian geniuses.

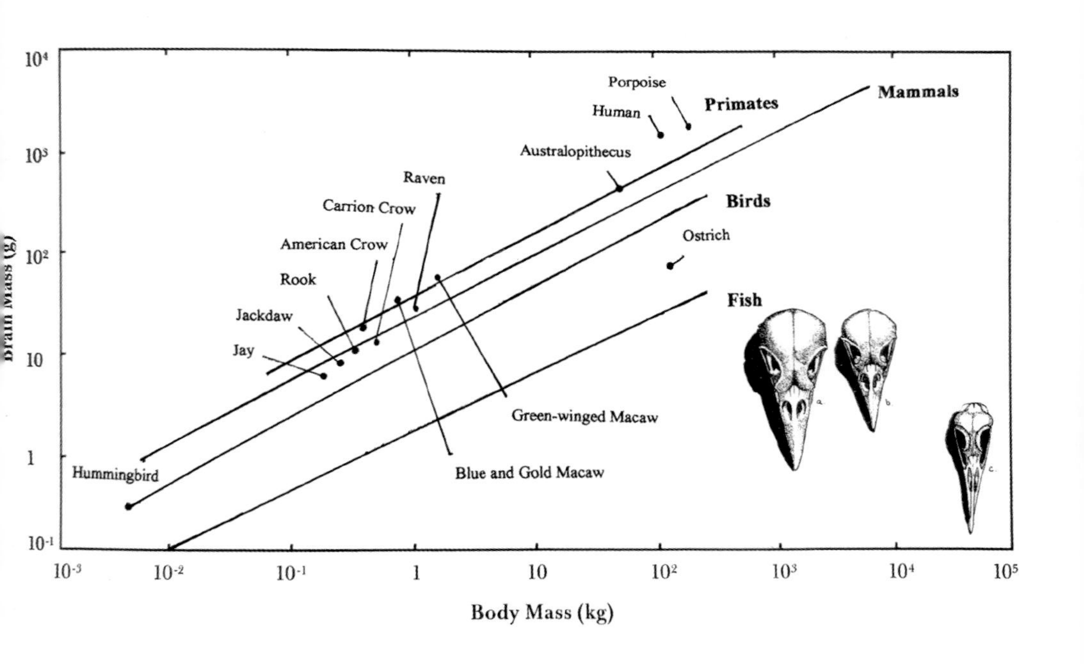

Diagram by Tony Angell illustrating brain to body mass ratios.

Corvids have a long life span and are sociable. These two factors, combined with their brain size, mean that they learn throughout their whole lives and not just by experiencing things themselves but through watching other birds too. Their brain has a large forebrain for assessing information; a hippocampus for spacial memory, the 'how did I get here and what are my senses telling me about my surroundings' part of the brain and an amygdala for assessing the emotion of how the bird felt in a situation and what happened there. The human brain has a hippocampus and an amygdala too. For many years it was thought that there was no cortex to the avian brain but a research paper in 2020 has shown that they have one, just not shaped like that in the mammalian brain. The organisation of the neurons is different but it functions in much the same way.

Corvids develop quite slowly, not breeding until they are between two and four years old. Juvenile birds stay around the nest territory watching and learning from their parents and other birds in the vicinity and using their brain to develop their understanding of how the world works. They have lots of opportunities to see other birds using tools and socially interacting. Learning what tastes good, what does not. What to fear as a threat, what to understand as harmless. Passing on of actual knowledge and not just automaton learnt behaviour seems to be a very singular trait of the corvid. Fledgelings need time to work things out; to survive, you need to be a quick learner. Being in a group supported by other young birds is a useful learning experience. For instance, a gang of juveniles might defend a carcass against theft by a group of older birds, whilst a single young bird might not.

Birds have large eyes, much larger than the eyeball that we can see from the outside of the skull. If you look at the skull in the brain/ body mass graphic, on the left is a raven, on the right is an American crow (slightly larger than our UK crow) and for contrast the skull in the corner is a cormorant. It is easy to see that the space for the eye is much larger than one might expect. The eye is full of sensors that take in visual information and send it to the right and left hemispheres of the brain. Bird hemispheres are not as connected to each other as ours but they can 'sleep' one half, whilst processing information in the other half. They have the facility to reconsider experiences just like us. They can take in a thought and assess whether to react to it or not and whether or not to send signals to the muscles to stimulate movement. This looping of ideas around the brain, from the forebrain to other areas and back, is one of the things that they share with humans, reflecting on the past and planning for the future.

Crow

Play

Young ravens do have a capacity to 'play'. It is well documented that they can invent single bird games like drop and catch (dropping something from high in the sky and trying to catch it before it hits the ground).

They also play games we might have played as children, like 'king of the castle'. Corvids are the most playful of birds and ravens are the most playful of corvids. Any new behaviour can be quickly learnt if it is fun, and this is vital for the building of experience, as is the case of the young of mammal species. Prof. Marzluff describes young ravens using pieces of wood to surf the wind high in the sky. The fact that they have amazing wings is immaterial, it is a fun thing to surf the wind on a piece of wood held in your claws.

Food

As omnivores, corvids will eat anything: frogs to field mice, carrion to caterpillars, berries to birds' eggs. Obviously the awareness of food potential starts in the nest and during the prolonged fledgeling/ juvenile stage. Learning is gradual. Jays love acorns and therefore the first lesson is 'this is an oak tree'. Over time they learn that a tiny sapling might have an acorn under it, their experience eventually helping them to only pull up oak saplings. Signalling by other birds to an event will be explored, as determined flying by other corvids may lead to a meal. Shouting and bluster by adult small birds could mean young in a nest, so hunt for it – there could be a meal there too. The information about process is stored and retained by corvids in such a way that they can recall and search images to help them find food. A raven 'couple' who have found a good food source will keep very quiet about it but if an unattached juvenile should find it, they will be quick to defend.

Like squirrels, corvids must cruise their home territory and decide how much effort and energy to expend on searching for food. Finding it once in a specific place does not mean that you will necessarily find it again.

Raven

Crow

At what point do you stop? Corvids have great ability to make food choices, such as weighing snails and whelks in the beak to decide if they are worth the effort of 'opening' them. The assessment of potential food for effort as against those easiest to open. The birds have a technique of dropping a shelled food source from a height and dropping it to smash it open. Experiments have shown that the birds will choose the heaviest ones to drop, meaning that they gain maximum speed by the time they reach the flat rock chosen as the target. The flatness is pertinent too, preventing the opened food falling back into the sea or the undergrowth. The height average for this shell opening technique is five metres; too high and the shells will shatter, meaning they have to pick the shell bits out of the edible bits. Crows have been seen dipping broken whelks in the sea to wash out

Carrion crows

any grit or bits. Intelligence means you are fuller quicker.

The supreme generalist when it comes to food, ravens will certainly feed heavily from those animals hunted and brought down by others but conversely are not above flipping a cow pat to get at the bugs underneath.

Co-operative foraging

There is a well-documented 'hit and run' technique that is used by ravens and magpies. A carnivore with its prey is targeted and one corvid will attack the catcher, forcing it to let go, whilst the other grabs what they had caught and flies off with it. It is a system that works on a cat with a mouse, a hawk with a frog or a dog with a rabbit. Usually, he who grabs the prize eats it! Pairs of corvids will harry a prey between them until one can strike and then the meal is shared. Furthermore, there are anecdotal stories of ravens indicating carcasses to larger mammals in the hope that when 'opened' they will have some scraps. Some ravens in Yellowstone National Park were tagged and it was noted that 43% of wolf kills were visited by tagged birds, who would travel up to ten miles to help finish what the wolf had started.

Caching

If there is too much food then the intelligent thing to do is cache it. All corvids cache but not all in the same way. Magpies, crows and rooks bury food in the ground, poking with their beaks and covering with soil or occasionally under grass or leaves. Stones might be added for extra protection. The birds are very alert to the prospect of theft and may even rebury if they think it necessary. There seems to be no problem finding a cache several days later, the birds locate it easily and rooks are particularly good at this, burying nuts and collecting them months later when they are hungry. (In America, when there is heavy snow, corvids can still locate their stash even when it is buried up to 50cm deep.) In caching experiments in the lab, 70% of birds found their own stash, with only 10% finding someone else's. Another laboratory research project appeared to show that if a cache was left near a prominent item like a rock and that rock was moved, the bird found the cache by adjusting the distance to where it would have been if the rock was back in the original position.

A study in the Netherlands seemed to show that if a corvid's close reference point was not visible, it would adjust to a point further away, perhaps a tree or a rock. If that was obscured, it was prepared to go further still to look at things like hills or streams, which would probably not have been altered by localised changes such as the weather.

Tool use

Everything from sticks to bits of wire and pebbles can be used in pursuit of a meal. As discussed previously, the young of corvids are fed for a considerable time after they fledge and the next clutch of young are being raised. In these family grouping situations they get lots of opportunity to see others using tools. Interestingly, the starting point for the work of one of the PhD students at the Comparative Cognition Laboratory in Madingley, Cambridge was Aesop's fable *The Crow and the Pitcher*. Would a rook really drop rocks into a pitcher of water to raise the level to a 'drinking point' it could reach? Well, after what you have read so far, you will not be surprised to find that the answer was yes, it would.

Professor Marzluff documents the woman in Sweden who one winter saw magpies on her lawn and started

Magpie

feeding them. Soon after, she noticed that they would follow her outside as she went past the window, so she threw out some food; days later they were pecking at the window and so she threw out some food. Within a short time, she heard the front doorbell ringing! It took the woman a while before she actually saw the magpie ringing the bell (which in this instance was its food tool). Of course, the point was that she had conditioned the magpies to come for food and they had conditioned her to give it when they attracted her attention. A truly symbiotic relationship.

Face recognition

Corvids are very good at face recognition and they have long memories, so upset them at your peril: your infamy will be passed down to future generations. The husband of the woman in Sweden

Jay

who fed the doorbell-ringing magpies told Professor Marzluff that he once pretended to throw something at them and the next day and every subsequent day the birds pooed on the windscreen of his car!

In Washington, Professor Marzluff ran an experiment to test the information gathering and face recognition retention of the corvids on campus. Birds were captured by someone in a caveman mask, the birds were kept for a short time and then released. The object of the exercise was to see if the corvids would 'recognise' the mask on campus later when someone was walking around wearing it. A control mask of Dick Cheney was also worn around campus but not worn by someone catching the birds, only the caveman mask was used for that.

Following the capture and release, the minute the birds saw the caveman mask they grouped and dive bombed the wearer, irrespective of whether the mask was worn upside down or a hat was worn on top. The Dick Cheney mask elicited no response whatsoever, as did the people who had actually worn the mask but went out without it.

The fascinating thing is that the team at Washington continued to bring out the caveman mask on campus for eight years, worn by different students, and not only did the wearers continue to be bombed and sworn at by the corvids but the numbers of birds doing so actually increased. This means that some of the birds doing the scolding were not even born when the 'incident' first happened and the antipathy to the caveman mask was passed on to subsequent generations.

Mimicry

Ravens can be trained to speak and will imitate their trainer's accent and tone very well indeed. According to his trainer, Jimmy the filmstar raven, who you will meet properly in the Art & Literature chapter, had a core repertoire of 50 'useful' words but knew many more. Naturalist Gerald Durrell kept several pet magpies who learnt to imitate the call of his maid to the house chickens at feeding time. Seemingly, when the magpies needed entertaining, they would call the chickens, who would come and then disperse unfed. The magpies would do it again and again and again; the chickens never learnt.

Finally, a word about an amazing facility in the UK. It is worth looking

Rook

on a search engine for videos made during work from the Comparative Cognition Laboratory in Madingley, Cambridge. It was founded and is run by Professor Nicola Clayton, who is world renowned for her work on the intelligence of corvids. Like Marzluff in the US, Professor Clayton thinks of the birds as 'feathered apes'.

At her laboratory she has twenty-five jays and seven rooks, all hand-reared by her. (The birds cannot be wild, as researchers would not know their previous experiences.)

With these corvid subjects she has been able to test and delineate their mental capabilities. The work of Clayton and her small team was seriously challenged in 2022, when the European Research Council decided it could no longer fund her research. Brexit has meant that grant funding has become more complicated for academics who have received support from Europe in the past. However, following an article in the *Guardian* and subsequently 358 leading academics signing a letter of support for her work, £500,000 was raised by public donations and the lab has been saved for the next five years at least.

This small laboratory is central to our changing understanding of animals. It was reported in *New Scientist* that studies conducted by Professor Clayton are 'part of a renaissance in our understanding of the cognition of other creatures... but there is still much more to learn.' Clayton told the *Guardian*: 'It's a privilege to get the opportunity to see inside their minds, and for them to trust us enough to share what they know with us.'

Jay

This is Nigel, the cat from across the green beside our house, and his story proves the fact that corvids never forget.

In 2021, there was a juvenile magpie from the group that lives in the trees next to our house who lost his tail feathers when Nigel pounced on him (we found the feathers in our garden).

Cut to the summer of 2022. Our upstairs studio has a window at the front and we were in there one morning when there was a massive amount of magpie swearing from outside. We hear the magpies from the trees all the time but this was just constant and very loud.

We looked out to see Nigel on the corner of the fence being shouted at by the tailless magpie, who perched on the corner of the workshop before flying down and bombing him. He then swung around and landed on the fence, harangued Nigel from behind, then flew around and back up to the corner. We watched this for some time and then, as I knew I would be starting this book soon, I thought I would take some pictures. Nigel got bored after 10 to 15 minutes of shouting and got down from the fence. The magpie followed him down the track beside the house, still swearing.

Raven

Raven

The raven, with a wingspan of 120-150cm, is a huge bird, larger even than a buzzard.

The profile is solid, a large rounded beak with feathers reaching down half its length. The throat feathers are thicker too and slightly more abundant than in other corvids. In flight the widely 'fingered' wings and diamond-shaped tail are easily recognised as belonging to a raven. It is also, as discussed in the previous chapter, one of the cleverest birds on the planet. This combination of scale and intellect helps make the raven an iconic bird in these islands. Its full title is the common or northern raven and it can survive in all kinds of terrain, covering a wide swathe of the northern hemisphere. It is very widely distributed in the UK, being found from top to bottom on the west side.

The raven is a very vocal creature, with a well-documented vocabulary of up to 30 sounds. The standard call is deep and easily recognised. Like other corvids it has a capacity for mimicry, which is, as you would expect, particularly noticeable in captive ravens.

This is a bird of the countryside – forests, mountains and uplands – meaning that it is not seen by the general public as much as the other UK corvids. It is a bird that likes to soar to great heights and has the potential to perform exciting aerobatics. This agility in the sky is used to great effect to mob raptors passing through its airspace, particularly in coastal regions.

Generally, ravens are residents in their territories but as with other corvids, non-breeders and young birds may spread their home ground a little wider. The raven is a solitary bird, most often seen singly or in pairs. Like other corvids, the pair bond is for life and the couple will stake a territory before they start breeding. Being large birds their nests are large and solid and constructed of sticks, lined with moss, mud and fur. They are early breeders, with the female laying three to seven blotchy blue-green eggs in early February. She will incubate them for approximately 18-21 days, with the large chicks taking 35-42 days to fledge and as is normal for corvids, staying with the parents for a further six months.

In past centuries, ravens were seen as a good thing within towns and villages as their scavenging, omnivorous habits were much appreciated in keeping the streets clean. On the other hand, they have been persecuted for their supposed attacks on young livestock. However, modern studies have in fact shown that in fact most young stock eaten had died of natural causes. The ultimate opportunist omnivore, the raven does well where it can easily reach food waste found in landfill, will take roadkill if resident by a road or different kinds of cereal if in farmland. They will also take the opportunity to clean up after other predators, such as foxes and badgers.

Owing to its size the raven has few natural predators of its own; eggs might be stolen from the nest by owls or pine martens, but the raven will defend its chicks and fledgelings with vigour. Today there are approximately 7,500 breeding pairs.

Ravens can have long lives, up to 20 years in the wild and approximately 40 in captivity. Perhaps the most famous and well-documented ravens in captivity are those to be found in the Tower of London. Naturally, there are many and various versions of how the ravens came to the Tower and who brought them there. One of the most often-quoted stories is that Charles II specified that they should be protected at the Tower after he was warned that both monarchy and Tower would fall if they should leave. However, it is considered by historians that the myth about the ravens is a construct from the Victorian period, without any factual basis.

A children's book called *London Town* from 1883 has the earliest depiction of the ravens at the Tower in an illustration by Thomas Crane and Elizabeth Houghton.

Above: Illustration from *London Town* (1883), the first depiction of the Tower ravens in print.

To this day the Tower has a cohort of seven resident ravens and a captive breeding scheme. England and the Tower are safe, at least for the foreseeable future.

Carrion Crow

Carrion Crow

The carrion crow (usually known in the UK as just 'the crow') is a serious-looking bird with a big brain.

Comparable in body size to the rook, it has a more rounded beak with fine feathers over the nostrils and a less shaggy profile, all together a tidier-looking bird. There is a faintly green and purple sheen to crow feathers too, redolent of the magpie's iridescence. It is considerably smaller than the raven by approximately 10cm in length and 50cm in wingspan.

When you are trying to identify birds, the statement that 'a flock of crows are probably rooks and a single rook is probably a crow' is often true, as crows are far less sociable than rooks. Naturally, there are exceptions to this: crows may socialise with others in roosts and whilst feeding, particularly in the winter, but as a general rule of thumb it does hold true. The call of the crow is distinctive, usually a three-beat kaaa, kaaa, kaaaaa, to the rook's single kaa. The crow also adds in a little dipping bow. Like other corvids, the crow has the capacity for mimicry.

The crow is a natural scavenger and frightened of nothing, neither humans nor other mammals that kill, like foxes or badgers. Ground feeders, they love nothing better than to wait for their moment and dodge in to feed on (as the name suggests) carrion.

They are not beyond working with others of their species to make kills of their own, taking small mammals and birds; as well as the ubiquitous egg stealing. Household waste is a good feeding ground for them and they are happy to be around humans in the city, on moorland or farmland. Their only natural predators are raptors such as goshawks, peregrine falcons and golden eagles.

They are truly omnivorous and are known to cache food for later: shreds of meat stored in trees and seeds buried in bark. They are not beyond stealing from the cached stores of other animals either. The ability to take advantage of whatever can be found makes crows unpopular with gamekeepers and farmers, who see eggs and chicks, or grains and early crops, attacked.

Crows are seasonal feeders, with the menu being dictated by need and what is available. Predation on gamebirds and other carrion comes to the fore, along with serious scavenging, when feeding their own brood. Insects and invertebrates are taken in the summer when there are more of them about, with grain and berries being an autumn and winter choice.

In common with other corvids, the nest is a stick-based and bulky affair, usually in a tall tree or even a cliff face or old building, if that is what is readily available, or occasionally nearer the ground. The breeding territory is large and, whilst they breed alone, they are not above grouping with nearby nesters and 'singletons' to mob a predator and see it off from the nesting area.

The female lays three to four greenish/bluish mottled brown eggs in early spring. She incubates for 18-20 days, fed by the attentive male. The young fledge at approximately 18-20 days.

Again, like other members of the crow family, last year's juveniles will often attend to support the next brood by scavenging and sharing food and generally assisting with 'nursery duties'.

Hooded Crow

Hooded Crow

Not to be confused with the totally black carrion crow (*Corvus corone*), 'the hoodie', as it is sometimes known (*Corvus cornix*), has exactly the same frame and stance but appears to be wearing a high-collared pale-grey bodywarmer with the black wings poking through. The throat and chest are black, accentuating the sense of a waistcoat done up across the stomach. The colouring of the feathers gives it an almost 'handknitted' look which is strikingly delicate and unusual.

For many decades the hooded crow was thought to be just a carrion crow in a different colouration, therefore it was originally classified as *Corvus corone cornix*. In 2002, however, with the support of DNA testing, scientists found that it was identical to *Corvus corone* but with one vital single gene responsible for their colouring

being different. This was thought to have come about geographically over 11,000 years ago, when the birds were divided into two isolated populations and a genetic mutation altered the plumage.

Unusually, hybrids of the two species are to be found and it would be expected that such offspring would be infertile. This is not the case, but as the few hybrid birds do not find others to mate with, the line stops. It would seem that this fertility could continue the hybridisation and study continues in this area.

Hooded crows chasing a buzzard.

The coastline of west Scotland, northern Ireland and the Isle of Man are the places to find the hooded crow these days. Like its close relative, the hoodie is a scavenger and stealer of eggs, with sea birds like cormorants and puffins a special favourite. The dropping of molluscs from a height to break them open is a technique shared with the carrion crow, so much so that in old Scottish Celtic the name for an empty sea urchin shell is 'crow's cup', a clear indication of their penchant for food from and around the sea.

Unlike family members further south, the hoodie nests from mid-May to mid-June. The rather shambolic stick nest, built by both partners (with seaweed woven in), is usually high in a tree, but cliff ledges and old buildings can be used.

There are four to six speckled blue/ brown eggs in a clutch, which the female will incubate for 17-19 days. Fledging takes place within three to five weeks and as with other corvids the youngsters will be fed for up to three weeks after fledging and continue to be part of the family group until the first winter is safely past.

Rook

Rook

If the other members of the crow family are glossy and prosperous looking, the rook resembles that dishevelled, shambolic uncle who turns up for family weddings and christenings.

With their sharp, pale, almost scaly-looking beaks and fluffy, shaggy belly feathers and 'trousers', there is an aura of the down at heel about rooks. The paleness of the bill is accentuated by the pale featherless skin immediately behind, which makes it seem longer. In juvenile rooks this skin is feathered which makes them harder to differentiate from crows (*Corvus corone*). These feathers around the beak fall out at about six months and then the white-beaked rook becomes very obvious.

Rooks are gregarious and like to be part of a flock, whilst crows are far more solitary. The old adage that 'a flock of crows are probably rooks and a single rook is probably a crow' is a helpful reminder of this fact. Whilst this is a big generalisation, it is true that during nesting, feeding and roosting rooks like to be part of a crowd. Crows, however, being very territorial, particularly during the breeding season, definitely do not like crowds.

A hanger or small group of tall trees is an absolute necessity for a tree-top rookery, as colonies of rooks are called. It is a noisy place when the birds are home with their fledged young. This caused one famous celebrity to complain that it made no difference who he was or that he had a mansion in the country; he was not allowed to take a shotgun to stop the constant racket!

Often seen marching around purposefully in arable or pastureland, they forage by thrusting those sharp and very strong beaks into the ground to feed on the grubs and invertebrates they find there. Grains, seeds and vegetables of all types are also a meal for rooks, as are fruits; after all, their Latin name is *Corvus frugilegus*, meaning raven 'fruit-gatherer'.

Rooks favour farmland, open countryside and small villages; they have never developed a true love of the heavily urban landscape like others of their tribe. That said, they will rifle through rubbish bins and scour the streets for an easy meal in the quiet of the early morning or at dusk and, being opportunists, they will also go for roadkill or the occasional small mammal. In the past farmers persecuted rooks for harming crops and thousands were shot annually. An understanding of the importance of the feeding of birds on pests in arable farming has since stopped the slaughter and it is estimated that there are at least a million breeding pairs in the UK (RSPB).

Their courtship display involves bowing, dropping of the wings and tail fanning. Rooks mate for life and rookery nests are often refurbished in a subsequent season, with new twigs on the outside and fresh earth, moss, grasses and leaves on the inside. Three to five eggs, which are greeny-blue with splotches of grey-brown, are laid at the end of March to early April. The female incubates them for 16-18 days and post-hatching for a further 32-33 days. During this whole period whilst she tends the nest, she and later the young, will be fed by the male. Once the chicks are safe to leave she will feed them too. Both parents bring food to the young in their throat pouch, the saggy, pale piece of skin under the beak, particularly noticeable in older birds. On fledging, the young will continue to be fed for up to six weeks.

Like other corvids, young rooks form large flocks in the autumn, together with unpaired juveniles and often including jackdaws. Rooks have a lifespan of approximately six years in the wild.

Magpie

Magpie

The handsome magpie, in its smart dinner jacket and long, iridescent tail feathers, may seem to be very different from other corvids.

Watch it move, however, and the characteristic strutting walk and latent power of the raven, the rook and the crow are all on show. The magpie is often hated for its infamous mythology, of which there is a considerable amount, and also its history of scavenging anything, particularly the young of other birds and mammals.

The name was probably originally simply 'pie', from the Latin *pica*, the prefix 'mag' being added around the 16th century, possibly derived from the woman's name Margaret, suggested by the nagging nature of the bird's call.

The ability of magpies to eat pest insects and rodents made them popular with farmers until the 1850s. Sadly, this was followed by heavy persecution from gamekeepers as the upper classes took to shooting and magpies were seen as a threat to game birds. Their numbers fell dramatically and this lasted until the end of WWII, when numbers began to increase, becoming stable during the 1990s. There are now thought to be about 600,000 breeding pairs (RSPB).

Like the fox before them, the magpie has found urban life a better fit for both lack of persecution and good food supplies. Being intelligent and quick to learn, living beside us is not a problem and they can breed slightly earlier, as the towns are warmer than the countryside. The shouty chatter and rattle of a small magpie colony in nearby trees can make sleeping on an early summer morning almost impossible. (Here speaks the voice of experience!) These days that sound is ubiquitous in the urban environment.

Ever the opportunist, a magpie will supplement its usual diet of insects, worms, small mammals, snails, autumn fruits of all sorts, grains and nuts with food from bird tables and anything supplied by garden bird lovers. They are always happy to feast on carrion roadkill.

If food is readily available, magpies will hoard by making a hole in the ground with the beak, burying the surplus and covering it with foliage or a stone.

It is not unusual in the world of corvids to see flocks of unpaired young birds and magpies are no exception to this. Sometimes they pair up in these flocks (they do pair for life) and will normally begin breeding at two years. Magpies will happily nest anywhere that appears suitable but prefer a high tree nest site, although they will nest in a hedge if nothing else is available. It can take up to two weeks for the couple to complete a nest, using twigs and small branches and lining it with soft moss, leaves and mud. Some magpies will build a dome over their nest to protect the young from marauding crows if these are a problem.

The laying of a single clutch starts from early April and usually there are five to eight blue-green eggs, heavily speckled with olive green splatters. The hen does all the incubation, which lasts 18-20 days. She starts sitting after a couple are laid, ensuring the earliest hatch first, meaning the strongest will be fed first if there is pressure on food when the eggs hatch.

The young are fed by both parents and fledge after approximately 27 days. Although the parents will continue to feed the fledglings for up to four weeks after they have left the nest, chick mortality is high and it is estimated by the RSPB that only 22 per cent will survive the first year. However, if they do survive, potentially they could live up to 21 years, though the average is three. The young birds, as with other corvids, stay in the parents' territory until the autumn, when they group in loose flocks for feeding and roosting.

With more magpies living in our urban environment, they have gained a bad reputation for causing the decline in songbird numbers across the UK. However, research by the RSPB and the British Trust for Ornithology found no evidence that predating of nests by magpies would have any significant effect on songbird populations. This fact needs to be stressed when new media spreads the lie that the opposite is true. This handsome bird needs our support to get beyond its bad press.

Chough

Chough

The rich carmine red beak and legs of the chough make it perhaps the handsomest of the UK corvids. It is also the rarest.

The chough (pronounced chuff to rhyme with ruff) was commonly known to many as the Cornish chough, which is not surprising as it features on the arms of both the county of Cornwall and the Duchy of Cornwall and there was, many years ago, a large population in the county.

Kent also has a strong link with the chough; it appears on the Canterbury coat of arms too and the reason is explained in full on pages 122-123 of the Myth and Legend chapter.

The last chough in Cornwall died in 1973, at which point they became officially extinct there. Twenty-eight years later there was a sighting of four to the west of the county and subsequently they bred and a tiny colony was established. From these small beginnings, by 2019 there were almost 100 birds in the area. Kent lost its choughs over 200 years ago but by 2023 it would seem that the birds are back, following many years of work from Kent Wildlife Trust, supported by the National Trust and White Cliffs Countryside.

Habitat is key to understanding the decline of the chough. Their feeding needs are very different from other corvids. Choughs are not opportunistic or adaptable feeders like ravens, crows or rooks. They quarter the ground in a very thorough search for insects and grubs. They can often be seen probing with their slim red beaks through animal dung for beetles or along the shoreline hunting for sand fleas. As you might expect, such particular feeders have been adversely affected by modern farming practices and climate change. Furthermore in farming, historically, they were heavily persecuted as a pest: unjustly in fact as they feed on insects and the grubs of the very pests the farmers needed to fight. Naturally as they were beautiful and were becoming rarer, they were also trapped for 'specimen' status and their eggs were prized by collectors too.

Cornwall and Kent have led the way in stewarding their coastline grasslands, using conservation methods to keep areas grazed but thriving and perfect for these handsome birds. This example has been followed elsewhere and with the help of the RSPB and Chough Study Groups there are now approximately 394 breeding pairs nationwide.

Choughs pair for a long time, probably for life, and they stay together even when not actively raising a brood. Roosting is in pairs too but is communal with other birds. The nest will be made from twigs, moss and grassy plant stems, occasionally held together with mud and lined with soft wool, available animal hair or thistledown. It may even be reused in subsequent years, with fresh lining, naturally. Favoured sites are caves, cliff ledges or crevices, old farm buildings and in special nest boxes, if provided. During the breeding season, they will roost near the nest and juveniles will often roost close by for up to two months after they have fledged. The family bond with young corvids has been discussed elsewhere and choughs are no exception, seeming to carry on beyond the normal timeframe for non-corvids.

In April, three to four eggs are laid at one to three-day intervals, with incubation starting after the third or fourth egg has been laid. The female does all the brooding to begin with, food being supplied by the male. They will share the task when it is safe for her to leave the young. Fledging is at six to seven weeks and after a further three weeks the young are self-sufficient but stay within range of the parents.

When they have grown more confident, the youngsters will join a juvenile flock, which may be some distance away. They will only leave this 'gang' when they are ready to breed, usually at between two and four years old. Many young birds are lost in the first six months after they fledge, but if they can get to breeding they would be expected to make it for another three years or so. Their maximum life expectancy is ten years.

Jackdaw

Jackdaw

The smallest of the corvid clan, the jackdaw exemplifies 'small man syndrome', overcompensating for its small stature by strutting, shouting and generally living life in the party lane.

Gregarious to a fault, flocks of them are often seen performing aerial tumbling, seemingly just for the fun of it. These aerobatic techniques are also used when they band together to drive out predator species. Jackdaws are everywhere, all at once: woodland, parkland, coast and in urban centres too. Like other corvids, they are highly intelligent and have learnt how to manage, wherever they live. Insects and invertebrates will be found on the farm, including from the backs of farm animals. Woodland provides mainly seeds, berries and small rodents. The urban environs furnish the scavenging omnivore with many opportunities and, of course, jackdaws will enjoy roadkill if it is on offer; they are well documented in this circumstance as feeding alongside rooks and crows.

Whereas the hooded crow has a very distinct grey plumage, the jackdaw grey is subtler; in some lights it is more of a grey sheen than an actual colour. The bird appears to be wearing a black mask, with a grey back to its head, its pale blue/white eye helping to create a rather garrulous and determined expression.

Jackdaws are monogamous, forming pair bonds in the first year but not mating until the second. Unlike other corvids, jackdaws habitually nest in crevices or small openings in buildings or holes in trees such as those abandoned by woodpeckers. At the coast, tiny, secure and sheltered ledges on cliffs are used. They will occasionally even re-use the nests of larger birds. In terms of how they nest, jackdaws tend to favour the communal approach, sometimes in the company of rooks. The nest is built by both parent birds from sticks and small twigs, lined with soil, animal hair, moss and other softer materials. Young unattached juveniles may help with the building too. These constructions cunningly fit any opening or platform and are ubiquitously seen on top of chimney pots.

One brood a year is raised in late April, the four to six eggs are glossy and pale blue/green in colour with dark brown splodgy speckles. All incubation is done by the female alone for 17-18 days. As with other corvids, the eggs are laid in succession, the nestlings fledging four to five weeks later, with parental help on hand with feeding in the subsequent weeks.

The family bond is strong and juveniles will often form communal flocks with parents and others until ready to breed themselves.

The jackdaws of these islands do not migrate in the winter but their numbers may increase here when winter migrants arrive, if the weather is bad in northern Europe.

Jay

Jay

Where to start with jays? Well clearly 'totally different' seems a good place, the bird for whom the term 'dandy' is a perfect fit.

The pale fawny pink back and breast, black and white tail and wing tips to rival the magpie, black droopy moustache down from the beak, topped off with a black striped head and black dotted eyeliner. Finally as if to say, 'you think that's a bit mad, look at this', a turquoise, black and white striped band at the top of the leading edge to the wings. Quite a look.

Ironically, being rather shy and living in broadleaved forests, in spite of the wonderful plumage, they are not often seen, although their harsh, raspy, shouty call is often heard.

The Latin name for a jay, adopted in 1760, is *Garrulus*, 'chattering or noisy', *glandarius*, 'of acorns' (more of acorns later). Its full title is the Eurasian jay, not to be confused with any of the 33 other jays worldwide and it is fairly common in deciduous woods. Like other corvids, it has joined the urban landscape too, wherever there are parks or wooded gardens, with numbers currently running at approximately 170,000 pairs nationally (RSPB). The natural shyness of the bird means that details of its life are not easily observed. However, we know it is rather solitary and does not form large flocks but gathers in small groups in spring – these could be young males hunting for a mate.

Jays pair for life but even 'couples' seem to be loners, although they

will work together to build the nest, feed the young and defend their territory. Nest building starts in April and the word most often used to describe the outside appearance is – scruffy. Usually built high in a tree fork or dense bush, with plenty of foliage cover, the nest is made of twigs, plant matter and animal hair to create a cup shape. The adults take much more care with the inside, using fine hair and roots to make a soft inner for their brood. The single clutch of 3-5 speckled blue/green eggs is laid and they take about 17 days to incubate. Fledging takes just over 20 days and, as with all corvids, they will be fed by the parents for several weeks afterwards. They are fully grown at one to two years of age.

Apart from the outrageous plumage, perhaps the most interesting fact about jays

concerns their relationship with oak trees. For most of the year jays could be described as feeding opportunists, eating insects (beetles, caterpillars), worms and small rodents as well as eggs and nestlings of other birds. In the autumn and winter months, berries, seeds, fruits and the much-relished acorn on offer. The jay, like other corvids, knows how to cache and retrieve food for leaner times and this is where their relationship with the oak comes in. Happy to fly miles outside their home range to find an oak tree, one bird could horde as many as 3,000 nuts over a winter (British Trust for Ornithology). Of course, if it fails to retrieve any of the cached acorns then a sapling may start to grow. Cleverly, in the summer jays know the sight of an oak sapling means there is an acorn underneath and

may retrieve it. The importance of deciduous broadleaved woodland as a favoured haunt of the jay is obvious.

You are more likely to see a jay in the autumn or winter, when the leaf canopy has dropped and they are diving between trees looking for acorns. They have an adapted gullet which helps them carry several at once and one in the bill too.

The name *glandarious* in the Latin term for the jay means 'of acorns', thus cementing their link to the tree. The failure of the acorn and seed harvest on the Continent can cause birds to flock to these islands but UK birds do not migrate. It is easy to understand that the loss of woodland would result in the loss of jays. On average, jays live for four years in the wild.

Huginn and Muninn sit on Odin's shoulders in an illustration from an 18th-century Icelandic manuscript.

Corvids in Myth and Legend

Corvids in Myth and Legend

Corvids are very important characters in myth and legend and there is enough knowledge about them to fill a whole book, let alone a chapter. Therefore, please consider this section to be something of a taster, to whet your enthusiasm for these most fascinating birds.

Raven

Greek legend has the raven acting as a messenger between the gods and mortals and as a symbol of bad luck. Apollo, for instance, scorched the raven black when it brought him the bad news that his love Coronis had been unfaithful.

In Christianity the raven is referenced as 'unclean'. In the Book of Genesis, it is stated that Noah released a raven to check if the flood was receding. The bird did not return and so he later released a dove who, after three attempts, returned with an olive leaf/twig, indicating that there was land. It has seemed strange to some scholars that the raven, bearing in mind Noah would have had a pair and that they bond for life, did not return. One hypothesis states that the greedy raven fed on the many bodies it found and could not be bothered to return. I rather favour another theory, which states that the raven and the dove were from two different iterations of the same story of the flood that got combined in the Bible version. The raven, far from abandoning the ark flew 'back and forth'. If you take that to mean back and forth to the ark, it could have returned to rest and then gone out again to look for land and did find it but when the stories were merged, the raven was the one who didn't come back. This thought has tied scholars for many, many generations to theories regarding the venal

12th-century fresco in the Abbey Church of Saint-Savin, France.

nature of ravens when compared to the purity of doves. If this interests you, I highly recommend studying the myriad theories out there in the Bible, the Talmud and the Quran, it is fascinating.

The raven is also credited in the Quran with showing Cain how to bury his brother Abel after he murdered him. Allah, as a mercy, sends two ravens to fight in front of Cain and one is killed. The victor uses its beak and claws to dig a hole and subsequently bury the loser. The resolution of the problem had been suggested and was accepted by Cain – this was the first burial of man.

There are few cultures worldwide that do not include the raven in one form or another, often as a harbinger of death and destruction or a trickster, gaining the upper hand by its cleverness.

From the sixth century, Odin was frequently depicted in northern European myths flanked by two birds. Later Norse mythology has two ravens (Huginn – 'thought' – and Muninn – 'memory') gathering information for Odin. The Vikings had ravens on their banners, whilst the Serbians had them as the subject of epic poems, telling of the death of a hero.

Left: Kwakwaka'wakw raven mask, c. 1801-1900, Brooklyn Museum.

Among the indigenous peoples of the Pacific Northwest coastal region, the raven features in two different areas, kept very separate, the creator raven or the more juvenile trickster raven, seen as sly, cunning and always hungry.

I found this legend when I was researching *The Owl Book* and used it there, but it is such a charming, simple tale that I see no reason not to use it here too. There are several old Inuit tales involving a raven and an owl. In some variants of the story, the owl and the raven make clothes for each other but this is my favourite, with the birds painting one another. At this time, both birds were a simple white and, being bored one day, decide to paint each other with black lamp oil. The raven goes first and makes a really good job of the owl, making lovely brush strokes over her breast and then dark wings flecked with white. The owl is

Above: *The Owl and the Raven*, stop-frame animation.

delighted, so much so that she gives the raven a new pair of Inuit kamiks (boots). Now it is the owl's turn to paint the raven, but the excited raven just wants to parade around in her new kamiks and will not stand still. The owl, in exasperation, throws the lamp oil over the raven, who has been shiny black ever since! This story can be seen in a delightful stop-frame animation using life-like seal fur puppets by Co Hoedeman.

Crow and hooded crow

The crow features in much Celtic mythology, although crows and ravens seem interchangeable. The warrior goddess Morrighan appears as a crow (Gaelic: *badb*) or is sometimes depicted with a trio of crows, hence the feeling that the goddess is watching you if you see a group of three crows together. Morrighan is principally known as the Goddess of War and in the 1867 essay *Revue Savoisienne* by M. Adolphe Pictet she is depicted with her two sisters, Neman and Macha, as sorceresses and witches, whose appearance could incite those fighting to greater feats of heroism or equally bring fear to the opposition. The *badb* form taken by Morrighan is in fact *Corvus cornix*, the hooded crow (known as the Royston crow or scarecrow in Ireland). The importance of the crow in the *Mabinogion* is evident, where Owain leads an army of crows. The *Popular Tales of the West Highlands* by John Francis Campbell contains many tales featuring the assistance of the same *badb*, hoodie or scarecrow.

The confusion over crow/raven in Celtic mythology may not have been helped by the stories about Brân, the king/giant of Welsh myths. The Welsh for corvid is *bran* and his full name is Bendigeidfran, which means 'blessed crow/raven'. The Irish Morrighan favoured the crow as her emblem but as you will see, the Brân legend eventually (certainly from the English perspective) favours the raven, though it could go either way. The ancient Celts believed that the centre of the soul was held in the head and so, when Brân was mortally wounded in battle, he made it clear he wanted his head removed and transported with his soldiers on their subsequent travels. Eventually, the White Mount (Tower Hill today) became the resting

Detail depicting a crow from the funeral banner of Lady Dai (Xin Zhui), 2nd century B.C.E., Hunan Provincial Museum, China.

place of the head, where the Tower's ravens still guard the country against all comers.

There are hundreds of Celtic myths involving crows and if this is an area you are particularly interested in, you will not be disappointed if you dig deeper.

An old rhyme about these wonderful birds, as they are seen by the farmer/gardener trying to plant seeds, runs: 'One for the pigeon, one for the crow, one to rot and one to grow.'

Interestingly, three-legged crows feature in the legends of Japan, known as Yatagarasu, China, known as Sanzuwu and Korean, known as Samjok-o. Both China and Korea connect crows to the sun, whilst the Japanese make Yatagarasu a symbol of guidance from the Gods; the Emperor Jimmu was said to have been led by him in his life journey.

North American indigenous peoples have always held the intelligence of the crow in great esteem and it is considered a harbinger of good luck, not bad. Some tribes have melded the crow and the raven together in their mythology but others see them as two species. The culture of some indigenous Native American peoples actually feature a Crow Clan and its totem: the Chippewa, Hopi, Menominee, Caddo, Tlingit and the Pueblo tribes of New Mexico all revere the crow. North America also has an indigenous tribe called Crow Nation, known to themselves as Apsáalooke (ap-saa-loo-cay) or 'children of the large-beaked bird'. (The original nature of the bird from which the Crow Nation gained its name is lost in the mists of time and it is quite possible that it was not a crow as we know it today. The name, however, still prevails.)

The Crow migrated from the east of the United States and are now based in the modern-day states of Montana, Wyoming and South Dakota. The seat of their government is on a reservation in south-east Montana.

In January 1871 in the *People's Literary Companion* the writer and abolitionist Henry Ward Beecher wrote: 'No wonder men despise crows. They are too much like men. Take off his wings, and put him in breeches, and crows make average men. Give men wings, and reduce their smartness a little, and many of them would be almost good enough to call crows.' (NB This is the actual comment he made, not that which is usually attributed to him.)

Rook

Rooks are gregarious, social birds. Large rookeries may contain many nests. If built high in the trees, this means the summer will be fine, whilst lower down signals rain and wind. An abandoned rookery signals the impending death of the landowner.

If you have ever wondered about 'four and twenty blackbirds baked in a pie', they were almost certainly rooks. Traditionally, Rook-shooting Day was 12 May, when the recently fledged rooks were unable to fly away, and rook pie was a delicacy in the rural countryside at that time of year. In Ireland, they were a staple meal for a poor family but were reported as being rather gamey and, depending on when they were shot, rather tough.

Above: Magpie illustration from *Pictorial Monograph of Birds* (1885) by Japanese painter Numata Kashu (1838-1901).

Magpie

In Ancient Greece magpies were sacred to Bacchus, the god of wine (I wonder if this was to do with the fact that you brayed like a magpie if you were drunk?). In ancient Rome, however, they were known for foretelling the future, rather like today (see the rhymes on the next page).

There is a connection between the plumage of the magpie and the crucifixion. It is a well-recognised part of folklore across Europe that corvids were all white originally and that they mourned the death of Christ at the crucifixion and turned black as a mark of respect.

The magpie, however, did not go into proper mourning and therefore it has black and white feathers. Another myth has the magpie not entering the Ark but sitting on a gunnell, getting wet and swearing. Stories of this type have meant condemnation in many cultures for the magpie and a reputation as an evil bird.

To ward off any evil connotations, one system of awareness of what was in store on seeing magpies is recorded as follows:

One for Sorrow,
Two for joy,
Three for a girl,
Four for a boy,
Five for silver,
Six for gold,
Seven for a secret never to be told.
Eight for a wish,
Nine for a kiss,
Ten a surprise you should be careful not to miss.
Eleven for health,
Twelve for wealth,
Thirteen beware it's the devil himself.

Or alternatively and shorter is:

One for sorrow,
Two for mirth,
Three for a wedding,
Four for a birth,
Five for rich,
Six for poor,
Seven for a witch, I can tell you no more.

To ward off 'sorrow' on seeing just one lone magpie, the salutations are many and various.

'Good morning, Mr Magpie, how are Mrs Magpie and all the other little magpies?'

'Hello, Jack, how's your brother?'

'Good morning, general' or 'Good morning, captain.'

'Good day, Mr. Hangman.'

Personally, I have always said, 'Good morrow, Mr. Magpie', and I doff an imaginary cap.

The most magpies I have ever seen together is 11, on a coastal heath in France. It was almost scary to see so many in one relatively small area.

Above: King Arthur and Sir Mordred by William Hatherell (1855-1928).

Chough

There are two myths concerning the chough and both are notable. Chronologically, the first concerns King Arthur and his death but of course, according to legend he didn't actually die, he just transformed into a chough. The red legs and beak of the bird act as a reminder of Arthur's bloody death. Naturally if all choughs could be King Arthur, it is considered very unlucky to kill a chough. Legends of King Arthur are synonymous with Cornwall and the chough, like Arthur, is one of the icons of the county.

The second myth concerns the death in December 1170 of St Thomas à Becket in Canterbury Cathedral. He was murdered by four knights of the royal court who thought they were acting on behalf of King Henry II. Henry was struggling with Becket, who had excommunicated several of the King's supporters, who also happened to be bishops. Hence the famous quote attributed to the king and overheard by the subsequent murderers. 'Will no one rid me of this turbulent priest?' (This quote can also be offered as 'troublesome priest' or 'meddlesome priest', but I have used turbulent as it is the version I learned at school.) The knights considered it an order and hurried off to do the king's bidding.

There was reportedly much blood in the cathedral after the murder. The legend says that a crow in the building witnessed the horror and dipped its beak and legs in the gore, transforming thereafter into the chough.

Above: The murder of St Thomas à Becket depicted in an early 13th-century manuscript, held at the British Library.

Jackdaw

Jackdaws, it seems, were predictors of all sorts of things: weather (see one and it will rain), a harbinger of death, an indicator of a new arrival if seen on a roof or a sign of good fortune if one crosses your path on your wedding day.

Ovid thought they brought rain, and Pliny liked them as they destroyed grasshopper eggs. In his Fables, Aesop thought the jackdaw stupid for going hungry whilst waiting for figs to ripen and for being vain enough to borrow feathers to make itself King of the Birds. The bird was later shamed when the feathers fell off. The Greeks thought jackdaws were foolish and, furthermore, that they were white until one of them mentioned to the god Apollo that his was wife was being unfaithful and

Apollo turned the white bird black. Confusingly, this legend is credited to the raven too!

There is a somewhat long-winded but amusing legend of Tom Moor Linen Draper concerning a jackdaw. Like many corvids, it learns to speak, saying: 'Who are you? Who are you? Tom Moor of Sackville Street.' His master, the said Tom Moor, likes a game of cards and the bird, by this time allowed free movement in the house, often watches the gamers. From the participants commenting on one very lucky player he learnt the phrase, 'Damn it, how he nicks them.' Later, when his master constantly lost, he learnt 'What brought you here? Bad company, by God.'

The tale moves through a slow descent into penury and finally, when all is lost and the master is destitute in the Fleet prison with his jackdaw by his side, he decides before he dies he must set his old friend free. He drags himself to the window and lets the bird out.

The jackdaw, being gregarious, joins a flock of other jackdaws and takes to raiding the Temple gardens, where the gardener is sowing plots for the season ahead. He and his fellow gardeners try shooting the birds, which fails miserably – the jackdaws just exit at the first sight of the gun. Someone recommends netting them. The gardener tries this and captures 15, including our hero. He takes them into an empty garret nearby to despatch them. Locking the doors and windows behind him, he lets them out of the net and they fly around the room. Tom Moor's jackdaw finds a spot in the rafters to watch what is happening.

The gardener catches the first bird, wrings its neck and throws it to the floor, shouting, 'There goes one.' As the man goes for a second bird, our hero quips, 'Damn it, how he nicks them' from the rafters. The gardener says to himself that the house is uninhabited and the door locked; he must have imagined the voice.

He grabs another jackdaw, whereupon 'Damn it, how he nicks them.' rings around the room again. The man looks up to see the bird with its mouth open and asks, 'Who are you?' The bird has the perfect answer, 'Tom Moor of Sackville Street.' 'The devil you are', says the man. 'What brought you here?' The bird replies, 'Bad company, by God, bad company, by God.'

The terrified gardener runs from the house, leaving the doors open and, of course, he is followed by the jubilant jackdaws, saved by their clever friend.

Jay

The jay does not have much of a presence in the myth and legend of anywhere, in spite of being the Eurasian jay and therefore covering a large landmass. There seems to have been an ancient community before the common era in Latvia, where the wing of a jay would sometimes be placed in the grave during burial, there is nothing else. However, in case you have ever wondered about the term 'jaywalking', it has an interesting derivation. It comes from America and originally the term was 'jay-driver', a person driving a horse-drawn carriage or early automobile, on the wrong side of the road. The implication being that they were a country bumpkin, not used to the ways of the city; in other words someone who knew no better, jay being a pejorative term for a stupid idiot.

The Junction City Union (Junction City, Kansas) from 28 June 1905 has the earliest mention of jay-driving but by October of that year *The Kansas City Star* was using a variation of the term on pedestrians too: 'Much annoyance would be obviated if people when meeting others going in the opposite direction would keep to the right and avoid collisions and being called a 'jay walker'. Finally, we get from this to the jay-walker in the 21st century: someone who carelessly or dangerously crosses the road at an inappropriate place or at an inappropriate time, often because they are concentrating on looking at their phone.

Above: Don't Jay Walk, 1937, US Library of Congress.

Raven by Mary Philpot.

Corvids in Art and Literature

Corvids in Art and Literature

'Then (when fine weather is impending) do the rooks, from their slender throats, utter clear cries, three or four times repeated and, stirred by some strange happiness, chatter continually to each other high amongst the leaves: then, too, do they love to revisit their small families in their cosy nests.'

Virgil (from *The Georgics*, 70-19 BC)

Twa Corbies / The Three Ravens

Two different views of the same story, with an extra bird in one. This is an exemplar of the way that a pre-printing oral tradition means that songs have a life of their own and can change as the mores of society change. *The Three Ravens* was first published in the song book *Melismata* compiled by Thomas Ravenscroft and published in 1611, whilst *Twa Corbies* was first published in Walter Scott's *Minstrelsy* in 1812. Both songs come from the oral tradition and it is certain that they date from well before their official publication.

When you start researching the *Twa Corbies* traditional ballad, you hit a problem of identity of the birds almost at once. Depending on where you look, they are *either* crows or ravens. The confusion seems to have come about because of *The Three Ravens* ballad and both deal with the same scenario but from a different viewpoint.

In both songs, carrion birds are discussing where they can get a meal and in both the body of a recently slain knight is up for consideration. In *The Three Ravens*, the birds admit that in fact the body is guarded by the knight's hawks, his hounds and finally his heavily pregnant wife in the form of a deer. The deer kisses the knight and gets the body onto her back and buries it in an 'earthen lake', whereupon she too dies. The birds conclude that it is wonderful that such love and fortitude wins over all adversity and they end the ballad without a meal. This could be interpreted as celebrating 'chivalric values' in the tale: love, loyalty and persistence unto death are to be honoured.

The tale as told in the *Twa Corbies* is completely different, although the beginning is the same. This time two birds are discussing breakfast and the dead knight lying nearby. In this scenario, they say that the hounds are off after other prey, as is the hawk. The lady has taken a new lover already and nobody cares about the dead knight or where he lies. They then describe exactly how they will eat him. The harshness and sharp observation make this a very taught read. The implications are obvious: 'life moves on'.

Personally, as a realist, I much prefer the Twa Corbies: life can be hard and is not wrapped in a permanent glow of love and loyalty. The text to both is here for you to decide which you prefer.

Above: *The Twa Corbies* by Arthur Rackham, c. 1919.

The Three Ravens

(This has a standard form of lines with a chorus and is traditionally written in this way after the first verse to save on the repetition.)

There were three rauens sat
on a tree,
downe a downe, hay downe, hay downe
There were three rauens sat
on a tree,
with a downe,
There were three rauens sat
on a tree,
They were as blacke as they
might be.
With a downe, derrie, derrie, derrie,
downe, downe.

The one of them said to his mate,
Where shall we our breakfast take?

Downe in yonder greene field,
There lies a Knight slain under his
shield,
His hounds they lie downe at his
feete,
So well they can their Master keepe,

His Hawkes they flie so eagerly,
There's no fowle dare him come nie

Downe there comes a fallow Doe,
As great with yong as she might goe,

She lift up his bloudy head,
And kist his wounds that were so red,

She got him up upon her backe,
And carried him to earthen lake,

She buried him before the prime,
She was dead her self ere euen-song
time.

God send euery gentleman,
Such haukes, such hounds, and such
a Leman.

Twa Corbies

As I was walking all alane,
I heard twa corbies making a mane;
The tane unto the t'other say,
'Where sall we gang and dine to-day?'

'In behint yon auld fail dyke,
I wot there lies a new-slain knight;
And naebody kens that he lies there,
But his hawk, his hound, and his lady
fair.

'His hound is to the hunting gane,
His hawk, to fetch the wild-fowl hame,
His lady's ta'en another mate,
So we may mak our dinner sweet.

'Ye'll sit on his white hause-bane,
And I'll pike out his bonny blue een.
Wi' ae lock o' his gowden hair,
We'll theek our nest when it grows bare.

'Mony a ane for him makes mane,
But nane sall ken whare he is gane:
O'er his white banes, when they are bare,
The wind sall blaw for evermair.'

Brief glossary

Twa Corbies – two carrion crows (or possibly ravens)
auld fail dyke – old turf wall
hause-bane – breast-bone
theek – feather
nane sall ken – none shall know

Right: Barnaby Rudge and Grip the Raven by Felix O. C. Darley, 1888.

Barnaby Rudge

Charles Dickens had a great love of ravens. The Dickens household over the years had three consecutive birds, all named Grip. They ruled the household and the ten Dickens children and assorted pets with a rod of iron, stealing food, pecking anyone who passed by and generally being very feisty.

Dickens' love of his corvids went as far as putting one (also called Grip) in *Barnaby Rudge*.

Above: Grip the Raven.

He was Barnaby's staunch companion and even went to Newgate Prison with him.

When Dickens toured America in 1842, he took Grip with him and whilst in Philadelphia they met Edgar Allan Poe, who was very taken with the bird and used it as inspiration for the next item in this chapter. When the third Grip died, Dickens had him stuffed and set above his desk. When Dickens died, Grip found his way across the Atlantic with different collectors and is now a resident of the Free Library of Philadelphia.

The Raven

Although *The Raven* (1845) by Edgar Allan Poe is perhaps his best-known work, Poe is also credited with being one of the creators of the first horror and detective stories. An American poet, critic and editor, for whom excellence of writing style was always at the heart of his work. He was a strange character to say the least; often offending those who could have had a really positive impact on his career. It could be said that he achieved success almost in spite of himself and he did, ultimately, die a pauper in very mysterious circumstances. In late 1849, he had recently returned to Baltimore where he disappeared for five days and was found seriously ill and clad in unfamiliar garments. He never regained full consciousness and died four days later.

The Raven made him the first worldwide literary star. The poem was a sensation, long before the days of media hyperbole. It was

The Raven by Graham Humphreys.

first published in 1845 under the pseudonym 'Quarles' in *The American Review*. The first publication credited to Poe was in the *New York Evening Mirror*, where the editor, N. P. Willis, described it as 'unsurpassed in English poetry for subtle conception, masterly ingenuity of versification, and consistent, sustaining of imaginative lift... It will stick to the memory of everybody who reads it.' Ultimately the critics were divided as to the merit of the poem but it gave Poe fame and did fulfil his requirements on writing it, of appealing to both the literary and the popular worlds.

The core element of *The Raven* is that the bird speaks and this, Poe admitted, had been inspired by the raven in Dickens' *Barnaby Rudge*. He further admitted that he had based the rhythm and metre on Elizabeth Barrett Browning's poem *Lady Geraldine's Courtship*. She later wrote to him: 'Your *Raven* has produced

Above: Illustration by Gustave Doré for the poem *The Raven*.

a sensation, a fit o' horror, here in England.'

In Europe too it caused excitement; the French poet Charles Baudelaire spent over a decade translating it and many illustrious illustrators have taken it on.

It is a long poem, so here is an extract to give you a flavour of its hypnotic qualities.

Extract from *The Raven* by Edgar Allan Poe:

Open here I flung the shutter, when, with many a flirt and flutter,
In there stepped a stately Raven of the saintly days of yore;
Not the least obeisance made he; not a minute stopped or stayed he;
But, with mien of lord or lady, perched above my chamber door—
Perched upon a bust of Pallas just above my chamber door—
Perched, and sat, and nothing more.

Then this ebony bird beguiling my sad fancy into smiling,
By the grave and stern decorum of the countenance it wore,
"Though thy crest be shorn and shaven, thou," I said, "art sure no craven,
Ghastly grim and ancient Raven wandering from the Nightly shore—
Tell me what thy lordly name is on the Night's Plutonian shore!"
Quoth the Raven "Nevermore."

Much I marvelled this ungainly fowl to hear discourse so plainly,
Though its answer little meaning— little relevancy bore;
For we cannot help agreeing that no living human being
Ever yet was blest with seeing bird above his chamber door—
Bird or beast upon the sculptured bust above his chamber door,
With such name as "Nevermore."

But the Raven, sitting lonely on the placid bust, spoke only
That one word, as if his soul in that one word he did outpour.
Nothing further then he uttered—not a feather then he fluttered—
Till I scarcely more than muttered "Other friends have flown before—
On the morrow *he* will leave me, as my hopes have flown before."
Then the bird said "Nevermore."

The Chough

A Cornish Piskey has lost his laugh and in a book from 1906, we see how King Arthur, in his chough persona, helps him find it.

From: *North Cornwall Fairies and Legends* by Enys Tregarthen

'When he crawled out from under the mallow, the first thing he saw on the Island facing him was the dark form of a great black chough. He was perched on the wall above the old arched doorway, gazing gravely in front of him.

'I am a poor little Piskey who has lost his laugh, and I am come to ask the Good King Arthur if he has seen it.' ...

...'Have patience,' said the chough kindly. 'Nothing is ever won by impatience. I have seen something very funny lately running about over the grass. It is like nothing I have ever seen before except in a Piskey's face when he laughs. ...'

...'It must have been my laugh you saw,' cried the Piskey - 'my dear little lost laugh that I have travelled so far to find. Where is it now, Good King Arthur?'

'It was here not long since,' answered the bird, who did not deny that he was Arthur the King. 'Why, there it is quite close to you,' pointing with his long-pointed beak to the most comical-looking thing you ever saw, on the grass a foot from where the Piskey was standing. 'It was a laugh gone mad,' as the chough said.'

Crow pyrography on cow skull by Jen Fry.

The Jackdaw of Rheims

In 1837 a series of articles were published in *New Monthly Magazine* called *The Ingoldsby Legends, or Mirth and Marvels* by Thomas Ingoldsby of Tappington Manor.

As the title suggests, it was a collection of legends, myths, poetry and even ghost stories but these were in fact written by a clergyman called Richard Harris Barnham, a priest at the Chapel Royal. His relatively light duties meant he could work on his stories for the magazine and although they had a basis in actual myths and legends, they were often funny and were perfect for reading aloud in a family setting. The tales became very popular and were collected into books from 1840.

Perhaps the most well known is *The Jackdaw of Rheims*, about a corvid who steals the cardinal's ring. It is a long tale with many verses, that starts with the jackdaw becoming a pet to the Cardinal and his monks. During a meal, the cardinal takes the ring off, puts it beside his plate and the jackdaw steals it.

There is an enormous hullabaloo, which ends with the Cardinal cursing the jackdaw, who leaves the scene of the crime. In the next verse, it is 24 hours later and the bird staggers back in a horrible state, lame, dishevelled and deeply sad. Here are the two subsequent verses so you can see what happens in the end.

Spoiler alert: the jackdaw gets away with it!

Left: Magic lantern slide illustrating the poem *The Jackdaw of Rheims*.

From *The Jackdaw of Rheims*

His eye so dim,
So wasted each limb,
That, heedless of grammar, they all cried, 'That's Him!
That's the scamp that has done this scandalous thing!
That's the thief that has got my Lord Cardinal's Ring!'
The poor little Jackdaw,
When the Monks he saw,
Feebly gave vent to the ghost of a caw;
And turn'd his bald head, as much as to say,
'Pray, be so good as to walk this way!'
Slower and slower
He limp'd on before,
Till they came to the back of the belfry door,
Where the first thing they saw,
Midst the sticks and the straw,
Was the Ring in the nest of that little Jackdaw!

Then the great Lord Cardinal call'd for his book,
And off that terrible curse he took;
The mute expression
Served in lieu of confession,
And, being thus coupled with full restitution,
The Jackdaw got plenary absolution!
When those words were heard,
That poor little bird
Was so changed in a moment, 'twas really absurd.
He grew sleek, and fat;

In addition to that,
A fresh crop of feathers came thick as a mat!
His tail waggled more
Even than before;
But no longer it wagg'd with an impudent air,
No longer he perch'd on the Cardinal's chair.
He hopp'd now about
With a gait devout;
At Matins, at Vespers, he never was out;
And, so far from any more pilfering deeds,
He always seem'd telling the Confessor's beads.
If any one lied, or if any one swore,
Or slumber'd in pray'r-time and happen'd to snore,
That good Jackdaw
Would give a great 'Caw!'
As much as to say, 'Don't do so any more!'
While many remark'd, as his manners they saw,
That they 'never had known such a pious Jackdaw!'
He long lived the pride
Of that country side,
And at last in the odour of sanctity died;
When, as words were too faint
His merits to paint,
The Conclave determined to make him a Saint;
And on newly-made Saints and Popes, as you know,
It's the custom, at Rome, new names to bestow,
So they canonized him by the name of Jim Crow!

It is unfortunate to note that the name 'Jim Crow' was used extensively during this period as a pejorative term for African Americans. Later in the century, white supremacy movements in the American South used it as a shorthand to cover laws that suppressed former slaves living in their midst.

Magpie by Catherine Hyde.

The Raven's Tomb

Walter de la Mare (1873-1956)

"Build me my tomb," the Raven said,
"Within the dark yew-tree,
So in the Autumn yewberries
Sad lamps may burn for me.
Summon the haunted beetle,
From twilight bud and bloom,
To drone a gloomy dirge for me
At dusk above my tomb.
Beseech ye too the glowworm
To rear her cloudy flame,
Where the small, flickering bats
resort,
Whistling in tears my name.
Let the round dew a whisper make,
Welling on twig and thorn;
And only the grey cock at night
Call through his silver horn.
And you, dear sisters, don your black
For ever and a day,
To show how true a raven
In his tomb is laid away."

Magpie by Jennifer Tetlow.

The Hollywood Film Star Raven

The world fell in love with Jimmy the raven in Frank Capra's *It's a Wonderful Life* (1946). His final film was *3 Ring Circus* (1954) and in between he appeared in over 1,000 films, with 22 of them fully credited at the end. Beloved of Capra, who gave him his first break in *You Can't Take it With You* (1938), Jimmy would appear in every subsequent film that the great director made.

On the set of *It's a Wonderful Life* it was the star actor, James (Jimmy) Stewart, who had to acquiesce to being called JS to stop the constant appearance of the corvid star when anyone called out 'Jimmy'. Stewart is quoted as saying during shooting: 'The raven is the smartest actor on set. They don't have to make as many retakes for him as for the rest of us.'

Curly Twiford owned Jimmy the raven and he thought his corvid actors the easiest to train. He estimated it would take Jimmy a week to learn a new word, two if it had two syllables. The birds repertoire of skills included typing on a typewriter, lighting a cigarette and turning over magazine pages. Curly said that in his estimation, Jimmy could perform anything that would be possible for a child of eight. (This agrees with the estimate of cognitive skill made by corvid specialists discussed in chapter one.)

As his popularity increased, MGM Studio had him insured for $10,000 and like the true 'actor' he was, he had 21 stand-ins who could cover for him when just a bird was required rather than one who could do specific movements or tricks. The most famous of these stand-ins was a raven called Koko who became known for his stoic ability to stay 'on mark' for as long as it took or until he became hypnotised by the lights and flew at them, whichever was the longer.

He made his last film in 1954 and then seems to disappear off the radar; Curly Twiford died two years later in 1956.

The Birds

Daphne du Maurier is frequently classified as a romantic novelist, however, she did have a penchant for exploring punishment and retribution; look no further than her best-known work, *Rebecca*. One of her most chilling and frightening creations in this genre is 'The Birds', from her 1952 collection *The Apple Tree* (reprinted in 1963 as *The Birds and Other Stories*).

The novella is set by du Maurier in her beloved Cornwall and the development of the story, of the speedy takeover of our world by the birds, almost aided by the apathy of the humans, is seen as an allegory of the way Britain ignored and then had to face down the rise of Germany before and during WWII.

It was later made into a film of the same name in 1963 by Alfred Hitchcock. The film, whilst gaining mixed reviews at the time, has since gone on to receive much acclaim, not least for its production without the ubiquitous CGI available to current film makers. The birds of the title were real and indeed wild, having been captured for the filming. They were loosely trained but understanding of the corvid brain was not as far developed as it is now and problems marshalling the avian actors and subsequent injuries to the cast seems to have caught the production team ill-prepared.

The female star, Tippi Hedren, received cuts to her face in the phonebox scene when glass was shattered by the bird attack and one of the ravens took an intense dislike to Rod Taylor, the male lead, and would hide and attack him the minute he arrived on set. Knowing what we now know about the facial recognition ability of ravens (and the ability to bear a grudge), this seems only too possible.

The nature of the story was changed in the film, with the themes being less general and more personal. It would seem that du Maurier was not impressed, as Hitchock moved the setting to California and put a more American spin on this scary tale. 'The Birds' is one of the most alarming short stories and if you have a chance do read it, you will never look at a bird in quite the same way again.

Crow: From the Life and Songs of the Crow by Ted Hughes, Faber and Faber, 1970.

On publication, Hughes himself described this as his masterpiece and said the poems used 'super-simple, super-ugly language'. There is certainly a hard immediacy about this particular collection. After the suicide of his wife Sylvia Plath in 1963, Hughes had a very barren creative period and *Crow*, written between 1966 and 1969, stirred his imagination and writing energy. This iteration of the book, published in 1970, was in fact just a selection from the pieces he had written so far for his original and much larger epic folktale project. The project had come to an abrupt halt following the suicide of his mistress Assia Wevill and her daughter Shura in March 1969. Their deaths put an end to his creative revival and *Crow: From the Life and Songs of the Crow* was the only salvageable section.

The narrative explores sex, religion but mainly death, as Crow searches the universe for his female Creator. Unfortunately these poems, including a small number of narrative links, is only two thirds of his original plan, which would have described an arc of exploration from the low point at the end of this book to the high point at the projected end, where Crow finds and marries his Creator.

Hughes made additions and deletions for subsequent reprints, the last of them for a 1997 edition. It has caused much controversy, however, mainly centring around its being unfinished, the brutality of the language, the provocative nature of the central character and the circumstances under which it was written.

Above: Raven pendant by Hannah Willow.

Crow's Fall by Ted Hughes

When Crow was white he decided the sun was too white.
He decided it glared much too whitely.
He decided to attack it and defeat it.

He got his strength flush and in full glitter.
He clawed and fluffed his rage up.
He aimed his beak direct at the sun's centre.

He laughed himself to the centre of himself

And attacked.

At his battle cry trees grew suddenly old,
Shadows flattened.

But the sun brightened —
It brightened, and Crow returned charred black.

He opened his mouth but what came out was charred black.

"Up there," he managed,
"Where white is black and black is white, I won."

Anabel's Raven

A much-loved children's book featuring a raven is *Anabel's Raven* by Joan Aitken, illustrated by Quentin Blake. To people of a certain era (now very definitely adults!) this tale is synonymous with the wonderful and multi-voiced Bernard Cribbens, who read the stories about Anabel and her raven Mortimer on BBC television programme *Jackanory* in the 1970s. The writing is mainly dialogue, so lends itself to reading aloud. The hilarity of the scrapes that Mortimer gets into are very innocent but beautifully created. Mortimer's one line, apart from 'caw', is 'nevermore' – I wonder where he got that from?

Collective terms for corvids

Chough

A chattering of choughs

Crow

A murder of crows
A congress of crows
A horde of crows
A muster of crows

Jackdaw

A clattering of jackdaws
A train of jackdaws

Jay

A band of jays
A party of jays
A scold of jays

Magpie

A mischief of magpies
A conventicle of magpies
A tiding of magpies
A charm of magpies

Raven

An unkindness of ravens
A constable of ravens
A conspiracy of ravens

Rook

A parliament of rooks
A storytelling of rooks
A building of rooks

Game of Thrones

The Three-eyed Raven is a character in both the books and the HBO television series, who lives beyond the Wall and first appears after Bran Stark falls from Winterfell tower. As previously mentioned, the Welsh word for Raven is *bran*. In the television series, when in human form the Three-eyed Raven was played by the enigmatic Max von Sydow. The raven looks out for Bran and acts as a guide in his journey north, finally becoming his mentor and helping him sharpen his Greensight abilities. These abilities become very important to the central plot as he visits visions of the past to help with the understanding of the present and future.

The ravens native to the lands of Westeros look like our ravens but have a stronger homing instinct. The birds use this heightened drive to carry messages between castles and other settlements by the Maesters of the Citadel. They are very crucial to many plotlines within the story and are revered for their strength and ability to speak. The Maesters train them to speak and to fly to specific castles as well as breeding them. Other birds, like pigeons and doves, can be trained too but the ravens are bigger, stronger, cleverer, can fly for longer and have the aerial ability and strength to defend themselves against attacks from hawks or other birds of prey.

Upstart Crow by Alastair Graham.

Ravens over Partrishow by Dru Marland.

Speaking Raven

I Grwyne Fawr

Sheep have spread their shrunken
woollens on barbed wire fences
wisps bleached white by winter sun
imitating lichen hung on blackthorn
twigs to dry

Delighted by pattern
the wind sends a pair of ravens overhead
It thinks they sound like frogs
but to me it's clear that they are
deep in conversation

Their topic a worsening in the weather
the move of the livestock market
from Abergavenny to Raglan
Or so I imagine,
not speaking raven

From *Map Reading for Beginners* by Deborah Harvey
(Indigo Dreams Publishing, 2014)

VII Palores

Sails spread against morning,
chancing the breaking spray of light,
a couple of choughs, pioneer lovers
seeking haven, their new court,
dreams of a dormant people
feathering their shoulders
The old ones knew the truth
A man with no tongue
will lose his land
so map our granite, tells its edges,
jig these clifftops
in your scarlet dancing boots,
lit firesticks blazing in your beaks,
scattering sparks

From *Map Reading for Beginners* by
Deborah Harvey (Indigo Dreams
Publishing, 2014)

Above: Mural in Ukraine.

Photo Credits and Artworks

Front cover: Tanya Ware.

Endpapers: Linocut by Jane Russ.

Back cover left to right: Sarah Hanson, David Hogg, Robin Morrison, Catriona Komlosi.

Introduction
Jane Russ: page 3.
Shutterstock: page 4-5.

Not Such a Bird Brain
Andy Wilson: page 6, 21.
Tony Angell: page 9
Claire Cameron: page 11,
Natasha Weyers-Gehring: page 13 (left).
Marie-Lan Taÿ Pamart Wikipedia: page 13 (right).
Hazel Mckay: page 14.
Kevin Sawford: page 17.
Robin Morrison: page 18.
Paul Fisher: page 20.
Jane Russ: page 22.

Raven
Robin Morrison: page 24, 27, 28 (top left and bottom left and right), 30-31.
Claire Cameron: page 28 (top right).
Colin on flickr: page 32.
Wikipedia public domain: page 33.

Carrion Crow
Claire Cameron: page 34, 38.
Paul Fisher: page 37.
Dod Morrison: page 39, 43.
Frances Crickmore: page 40.
Kevin Sawford: page 41.
Flickr: page 42.
Eric Webb: page 44.
Hazel Mckay: page 45.

Hooded Crow
Claire Cameron: page 46, 54, 55.
Kevin Sawford: page 48-49, 50.
Hugh Linn: page 51.
Linda Thompson: page 52.
Hazel Mckay: page 53.

Rook
Andy Wilson: page 56.
Trevor Clifford: page 59.
Kevin Sawford: page 61, 67.
Simon Nicol: page 62.
Margaret Holland: page 63.
Catriona Komlosi: page 64.
Hugh Linn: page 65.
Natasha Weyers-Gehring: page 66.

Magpie
Trevor Clifford: page 68.
David Hogg: page 71.
Kevin Sawford: page 72, 73.
Kevin Pigney: page 75.
Dod Morrison: page 76 (top left).
Robin Morrison: page 76 (top right).
Kevin Sawford: page 76 (bottom left).
Jacob W. Frank, Flickr: page 76 (bottom right).

Chough
Robin Morrison: page 78, 88.
Hugh Linn: page 81.
Wikimedia: page 80.
Margaret Holland: page 82.
Ian Preston: page 83, 87, 89.
Robin Morrison: page 84, 85.

Jackdaw
Trevor Clifford: page 90.
Kevin Sawford: page 93, 98.
Sarah Hanson: page 94 (left).
Robin Morrison: page 94 (top and bottom right), 96 (bottom left), 99.
Sarah Hanson: page 95.
Hazel Mckay: page 96 (top right).
Patrick Clements, Flickr: page 96 (top right).
Claire Cameron: page 96 (bottom right).
Andy Wilson: page 97.

Jay
Robin Morrison: page 100.
Kevin Pigney: page 103.
Andy Wilson: page 104.
Barbara Allen: page 105 (left).
Wikipedia: page 105 (right).
Beverley Thain: page 106.
Claire Cameron: page 107.
Kevin Sawford: page 108.
Margaret Holland: page 109.

Corvids in Myth and Legend
Wikipedia, public domain: page 110, 122, 127.
Flickr Simon Cope: page 113.
Brooklyn Museum, public domain: page 114.
Public domain: page 115, 117, 120, 123.
Davena Hooson: page 124.

Corvids in Art and Literature
Mary Philpot: page 128.
Wikipedia public domain: page 131, 146, 147.
Public domain: page 133.
Free Library of Philadelphia: page 134.
Graham Humphreys – grahamhumphreys. com: page 135.
Guttenberg, public domain: page 136.
Jen Fry: page 139.
Dutch Virtual Magic Lantern Museum, Henc de Roo: page 141.

Seat at bus stop in the USA shared on a crow-based Facebook page.

Catherine Hyde: page 144.
Jennifer Tetlow: page 145.
Hannah Willow: page 149.
Alastair Graham: page 153.
Dru Marland: page 154.
Wikimapia: page 157.
Facebook: page 159.

Every effort has been made to trace copyright holders of material and acknowledge permission for this publication. The publisher apologises for any errors or omissions to rights holders and would be grateful for notification of credits and corrections that should be included in future reprints or editions of this book.

Acknowledgements

The photographers for this project have really surprised me. I have worked with most of them for many years; mainly with the mammal volumes in this series but I had no idea they were all so keen on birds too! Thank you all so much... as always you came up trumps and this book is a photographic joy.

The artists, sculptors, painters, jewellers and poets all rose to the challenge and for that I am very grateful and humbled by the amazing talent on show. Thank you all.

This book has taken longer than usual to come to print. Therefore, I would like to thank all the chums I have bored to destruction with, 'surprising facts about corvids'. Your forbearance is much appreciated.

The Crow Family Book
Published in Great Britain in 2023 by Graffeg Limited.

Graffeg Limited, 24 Stradey Park Business Centre, Mwrwg Road, Llangennech, Llanelli, Carmarthenshire, SA14 8YP, Wales, UK.
Tel: 01554 824000. www.graffeg.com.

Jane Russ is hereby identified as the author of this work in accordance with section 77 of the Copyright, Designs and Patents Act 1988.

A CIP Catalogue record for this book is available from the British Library.

Printed in China TT300623

ISBN 9781802583564

1 2 3 4 5 6 7 8 9

Books in the series

www.graffeg.com